D0805510

On Remembrance Day

On Remembrance Day

ELEANOR CREASEY

DUNDURN
TORONTO

Editor: Allison Hirst
Design: Courtney Horner
Printer: Friesens

Library and Archives Canada Cataloguing in Publication

Creasey, Eleanor, author
On Remembrance Day / Eleanor Creasey.

Issued in print and electronic formats.
ISBN 978-1-4597-2166-1

1. Remembrance Day (Canada)--Juvenile literature. I. Title.

D680.C2C74 2014   j394.264   C2014-902132-1
                                            C2014-902133-X

    1   2   3   4   5   18   17   16   15   14

We acknowledge the support of the **Canada Council for the Arts** and the **Ontario Arts Council** for our publishing program. We also acknowledge the financial support of the **Government of Canada** through the **Canada Book Fund** and **Livres Canada Books**, and the **Government of Ontario** through the **Ontario Book Publishing Tax Credit** and the **Ontario Media Development Corporation**.

Care has been taken to trace the ownership of copyright material used in this book. The author and the publisher welcome any information enabling them to rectify any references or credits in subsequent editions.
J. Kirk Howard, President

The publisher is not responsible for websites or their content unless they are owned by the publisher.

Printed and bound in Canada.

Cover design by Jesse Hooper.

Cover image (poppies) courtesy of © dynasoar/iStock. All other cover images by Peter Creascy.

Visit us at
Dundurn.com | @dundurnpress | Facebook.com/dundurnpress | Pinterest.com/Dundurnpress

Dundurn
3 Church Street, Suite 500
Toronto, Ontario, Canada
M5E 1M2

Gazelle Book Services Limited
White Cross Mills
High Town, Lancaster, England
LA1 4XS

Dundurn
2250 Military Road
Tonawanda, NY
U.S.A. 14150

In remembrance of Private James Gordon Hill, 11 Field Ambulance, who was my great-uncle. He died during the First World War and is buried in Rouen, France. His most precious gift is remembered with respect and gratitude.

With gratitude to Gordon McKenzie Hill, my dad, who served with honour in the Royal Canadian Air Force in the Second World War and returned to live his life as a proud Canadian. The gift of your return is our constant celebration.

In memory of my mother, Helen Plasteras Hill.

For Peter, my partner in remembering.

And for Erin, David, Julie, and Helen: Hold high the torch!

The Tomb of the Unknown Soldier in Ottawa, Ontario.

A Day for Remembrance

Each year, late in the fall, when winter seems only a breath away, when the leaves have turned from green to yellow and orange and red and then blown away, and when the last Halloween pumpkin has said its final farewell, Canadians remember.

At the beginning of November, you will start to see people wearing small red poppies on their coats and jackets. Each day, more and more people will put on a poppy, until by November 11 it seems like there are millions of poppies out there. Veterans wear them, armed forces members wear them, business people wear them, ministers and doctors and teachers wear them. Even school kids wear them.

Canadians wear poppies and we remember. But what do we remember? And why? In this book, many of the customs and traditions of Canada's Remembrance Day will be explained. It is hoped that students, parents, and teachers will find the explanations beneficial as they prepare for this special day.

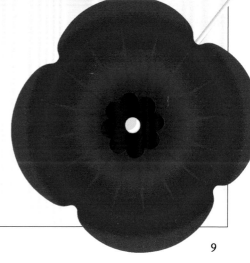

THE 11TH HOUR OF THE 11TH DAY OF THE 11TH MONTH

In Canada, we set aside one day each year, November 11, as Remembrance Day. The reason we observe Remembrance Day on this particular day is that it was on November 11, 1918, at 11:00 in the morning, that the armistice that ended the First World War came into effect. The armistice was an agreement between the Germans and the Allies to end the fighting. Later, a treaty was signed by all nations involved that set out the terms for peace.

The first Remembrance Day was observed a year after the armistice, on November 11, 1919. At the time it was called Armistice Day. The name was officially changed to "Remembrance Day" by a Canadian government bill passed in 1931.

Today, all across Canada, people attend ceremonies on Remembrance Day to honour all those who have been killed in service to our country.

In Flanders Fields the Poppies Blow ...

During the First World War, soldiers in northern Europe noticed that, every spring, red poppies grew in the battlefields and around the graves where their fallen comrades were buried. These poppies inspired Canadian physician Lieutenant Colonel John McCrae to write the poem "In Flanders Fields."

There are a variety of stories about why we came to wear poppies for Remembrance Day. Some believe that it was an American woman, Moina Michael, who, inspired by the poem by John McCrae, came up with the idea to use cloth poppies as symbolic reminders of those who had not returned home. Her idea was not very successful at first, but a few years later a French woman, Anna Guérin, began to promote the idea of selling the poppies to support worthy causes related to the war. She travelled to many countries, including Canada, where she met with representatives of the Great War Veterans' Association of Canada. This group decided to name the poppy as their national flower of Remembrance on July 5, 1921. Starting in 1922, disabled war veterans began making the poppies, sponsored by the Canadian government. Today, the Royal Canadian Legion produces and sells the poppies we all wear on Remembrance Day.

Although poppies are beautiful flowers that grow in many colours, the Remembrance Day poppy is always bright red with a black centre. We wear the red poppy to show honour and respect for the dead of all wars, including the First and Second World Wars and the Korean Conflict, as well as those who died in Afghanistan, and all the other places in the world where Canadian armed forces have been involved in both war and peacekeeping.

The poppy is always worn on the left side of the chest, over the heart.

CANADA'S WAR MEMORIALS

Almost every town and city in Canada has a cenotaph or war memorial in recognition of the fallen members of the Canadian armed forces. A cenotaph, or war memorial, is a monument dedicated to a person or a number of people who are buried in another place. These monuments are most frequently erected in honour of those who have died in war. In Ottawa, Canada's capital city, the National War Memorial and the Tomb of the Unknown Soldier, which lies at its base, are dedicated to the memory of all Canadians who have offered their lives for our country.

Across Canada, there are almost 6,300 different memorials or cenotaphs. They differ greatly in size and design, but just about every village, town, and city has at least one. Often the names of the fallen from that particular place are inscribed on the memorial.

On Remembrance Day, we gather at war memorials and cenotaphs across the country to pay our respects. (Right) War Memorial in Charlottetown, Prince Edward Island.

THE NATIONAL WAR MEMORIAL

In 1925, the Government of Canada held a competition to choose a design for a National War Memorial to honour all the Canadians killed in the First World War. The winning design by Mr. Vernon March was called *The Response*. The memorial was officially unveiled by King George VI on May 21, 1939, at exactly eleven o'clock in the morning.

The Response is located in Ottawa's Confederation Square, very close to the Houses of Parliament. The National War Memorial stands as a permanent way of remembering our fallen men and women. Thousands of people visit the site throughout the year. Confederation Square is also the site of our National Remembrance Day Ceremony, which is held every November 11.

On Remembrance Day, we remember those who have offered or given their lives in war. (Right) The National War Memorial, Ottawa, Ontario.

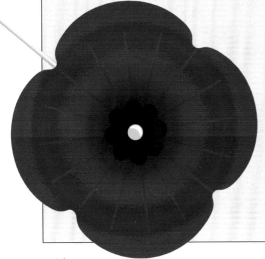

Photo by Peter Creasey.

On Remembrance Day, poppies are placed on tombs and memorials in honour of the fallen.

THE TOMB OF THE UNKNOWN SOLDIER

The Tomb of the Unknown Soldier was added to the base of the War Memorial in the year 2000. It contains the remains of a Canadian soldier who could not be identified. This soldier died in France during the First World War and was buried in a cemetery near Vimy Ridge, a place where Canadians fought and won a very important battle. The soldier's remains were returned to Canada in 2000 and placed in this tomb. The tomb represents our respect for all the fallen, from every war and from every branch of service.

When the Tomb of the Unknown Soldier was placed at the base of the War Memorial, a new tradition developed. At the end of the National Remembrance Day Ceremony, people started to remove their red poppies and place them on the top of the tomb. Now this happens every year. It is a sign of respect for all the fallen, even those whose names we will never know.

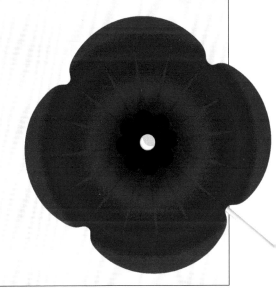

How Do We Pay Tribute to Our Fallen?

On Remembrance Day, Canadians join together at many places and in different ways to pay their respects to our war dead.

There are a variety of ways that Remembrance Day ceremonies can be held and each has significance. Simple and heartfelt ceremonies are within the capacity of the smallest school or community, and we see many of these on Remembrance Day.

The Government of Canada leads the National Remembrance Day Ceremony at the National War Memorial in Ottawa. This service is attended by government officials, including the governor general and the prime minister. Student winners of an essay contest sponsored by the Royal Canadian Legion represent Canada's young people, and one mother, known as the Silver Cross Mother, represents the parents of the fallen. Veterans and members of the military and their families are also part of this event, along with thousands of ordinary Canadians. The service is televised and available for everyone in the country to watch.

Although the specifics can vary from one place to another, some things typically happen at each Remembrance Day ceremony.

Songs and Recitations

The Canadian national anthem, "O Canada," is sung during the ceremony. The National Remembrance Day Ceremony concludes with the singing of "God Save the Queen."

Ceremonies may also include poems and songs that reflect our appreciation and respect for those who lost their lives in war. One of the most well-known poems we hear is "In Flanders Fields," which was written by Canadian poet John McCrae. It is often presented either as a reading or recitation (a group saying the words together), or in song. Here is how it begins:

> *In Flanders fields the poppies blow*
> *Between the crosses, row on row,*
> *That mark our place; and in the sky*
> *The larks, still bravely singing, fly*
> *Scarce heard amid the guns below.*
>
> *We are the Dead. Short days ago*
> *We lived, felt dawn, saw sunset glow,*
> *Loved and were loved, and now we lie*
> *In Flanders fields.*

Another poem often presented in full or in part is "For the Fallen" by British poet Laurence Binyon:

> *They shall grow not old, as we that are left grow old:*
> *Age shall not weary them, nor the years condemn.*
> *At the going down of the sun and in the morning*
> *We will remember them.*

At the end of this poem, the audience responds by repeating the last line together: "We will remember them."

Laying Wreaths

At many Remembrance Day ceremonies, a wreath or several wreaths are placed as another way of honouring the fallen, a sign of respect and remembrance. At the National Remembrance Day Ceremony, many groups lay a wreath at the conclusion of the ceremony. In schools, often one wreath is prominently displayed at some point in the program.

During the rest of the year, whenever notable dignitaries, such as the Queen, visit Canada, they always visit the War Memorial and lay a wreath. And, when our governor general or prime minister visit other countries, he or she places a wreath at the war memorials in those nations on behalf of the people of Canada.

Photo by Peter Creasey.

On Remembrance Day, wreaths are placed to honour the fallen.

PARADES AND VIGILS

Some of the more elaborate events, of which the National Remembrance Day Ceremony in Ottawa is one, include marches of military personnel, veterans, prominent participants, and bands to the location of the ceremony. There is also often another parade at the end of the ceremony. For fifteen minutes prior to the commencement of the National Ceremony, a vigil is held, with one member from each of the three branches of the armed forces, a member of the RCMP (Royal Canadian Mounted Police), and a nurse, taking their places to hold the vigil. In this ceremony, immediately following the Silence, a bagpiper plays the "Piper's Lament," and then the trumpet plays the "Rouse." During the ceremony, a 21-gun memorial salute is held. Poems are read, prayers are offered, songs and hymns are sung, wreaths are laid, and usually there is a "fly past" of airplanes from Canada's Royal Canadian Air Force, which are sometimes accompanied by vintage planes from the war eras.

On Remembrance Day, marches and parades are part of many ceremonies.

On Remembrance Day, we observe The Silence.

THE SILENCE

On the day of the ceremony, at exactly 11:00 a.m., a bugler plays the "Last Post." This is immediately followed by a two-minute silence. The Silence is a time when all people in a gathering are completely silent for a time. They stand and they do not talk and they try to be as still as possible. Sometimes people bow their heads and close their eyes during the Silence. The end of the two minutes is indicated by a trumpeter playing the bugle call "The Rouse."

We observe the Silence (also known as the Moment of Silence) in order to honour the memory of those who have died for us and for our country. The Silence is a simple but powerful way to show our respect and sadness, and to honour the memory of these great and generous Canadians.

In the beginning, the Silence was observed at 11:00 a.m. on the 11th day of the 11th month of the year, and it was two minutes long. In official ceremonies, this is still the time and length of the Silence. Sometimes the order of the ceremony is changed in order to have the Silence occur at this particular time.

Because many schools in Canada are closed on November 11 to observe the holiday, the Silence is observed as part of the Remembrance Day Assembly (usually held on the last school day before the holiday). If possible, the Silence is held at 11:00 a.m. on the day of the assembly.

Some stores and other public places may be open on November 11, so many times the Silence will be announced over a loudspeaker so that people there will not forget. When the announcement is made, everyone who is in the store or other place is asked to observe the Silence.

WARS AND ACTIONS IN WHICH CANADA HAS PARTICIPATED

Canada has been involved in several wars since the First World War. Canadian men and women have fought for their country along with their allies. *Allies* are countries that believe in the same philosophy as we do and with whom we work together. Canada has usually been allied with the United States and Great Britain, among other countries. Here are some of the areas and some of the battles where Canadians fought in wars. A *Theatre of Operation* is a large area or country where a number of battles took place.

FIRST WORLD WAR (1914–1918)

Theatres of Operation: The Atlantic Ocean, Great Britain (Home Defence), Belgian Coast, France and Belgium, the Mediterranean, Mesopotamia, the Pacific Ocean, Dardanelles, Macedonia, Egypt and Palestine, German East Africa, Italy, Persia, North Russia, South Russia, and Siberia.

Some famous battles in which the Canadian Expeditionary Force participated: Battle of Ypres, Battle of Verdun, Battle of Beaumont Hamel, Battle of the Somme, Battle of Vimy Ridge, Battle of Passchendaele, and Battle of Amiens.

Notes: In 1914, the population of Canada was only 7,879,000. Of these, Canada provided 628,736 participants to the First World War. This was nearly 10 percent of the population at that time. Of these, 66,573 died. It is said that every Canadian family lost at least one member in the First World War.

James Gordon Hill, a medic with the Canadian Army Medical Corps, one of those to whom this book is dedicated, was one of these. He was just 25 years old when he died on November 28, 1916.

(Right) The final resting place of Private James Gordon Hill, a medic with the Canadian Army Medical Corps who was killed during the First World War. St. Sever Cemetery Extension in Rouen, France.

On Remembrance Day, we think about some of the faraway places where Canadian soldiers, airmen, and sailors fought, and where many died. This is the entrance to the famous Juno Beach, where the Canadian Forces landed on D-Day during the Second World War. Courseulles-sur-Mer, Normandy, France.

SECOND WORLD WAR (1939–1945)

Theatres of Operation: Dunkirk, Dieppe, Fortress Europe, Northwest Europe, Southern France, Normandy, Bourguébus Ridge, Falaise, Channel Ports, The Scheldt, The Rhineland, The Rhine, Caen, and Hong Kong and Southeast Asia.
Some of the famous battles involving Canadians: Dieppe, D-Day, Battle of the Atlantic, Mediterranean Campaign, Liberation of the Netherlands, and Battle of Britain.
Note: During the Second World War, over one million Canadians participated in the armed forces. Of these, 44,927 died.

KOREA (1950–1953)

Major battle: Battle of Kapyong
Notes: The war in Korea included 26,791 Canadians, of whom 516 died. The resolution of the Korean War was an armistice, an agreement to stop fighting, but no official treaty was ever signed. There are incidents on the Korean peninsula that continue to this day.

United Nations Peacekeeping (1956–Present Day)

Since the Suez Crisis of 1956, Canada has participated in many United Nations peacekeeping operations, including in Cyprus, Egypt, the Congo, and Rwanda. As of 2014, 121 Canadians have died during these efforts.

Kuwait (1991)

Canada participated in the allied coalition to enforce United Nations sanctions against Iraq. Canadian forces experienced no loss of life in this conflict.

Afghanistan (2001–2014)

One hundred and fifty-eight members of the Canadian military died in the war in Afghanistan or in support of the war. One of these casualties was Captain Nichola Goddard, the first Canadian female combat soldier killed while fighting. Below is a photo of her gravestone, which is located in the National Military section of the Beechwood Cemetery in Ottawa. Four Canadian civilians and one senior foreign affairs official were also killed in Afghanistan.

Photo by Peter Creasey.

The gravestone marking the final resting place of Captain Nichola Goddard, the first Canadian female combat soldier killed while fighting in Afghanistan.

WHY WE REMEMBER

WHAT IS REMEMBRANCE?

Remembrance is about learning what happened years ago and reflecting on the sacrifices made for us by others. Most of us were not around to experience the wars of the twentieth century that Canada was involved in, but by studying the past and learning about more recent military actions, we can come to know how these wars influenced the country that we live in today. We can also learn what life was like for the men and women who lived during those times of war and find out about the people who died serving our country.

WHAT IS GRATITUDE?

Gratitude is thankfulness. We are thankful to the members of the armed forces who fought for the freedoms we enjoy today.

WHAT IS RESPECT AND HOW DO WE SHOW RESPECT ON REMEMBRANCE DAY?

To *respect* means to admire, to have a high opinion of, and to regard with special consideration. On Remembrance Day we show respect to the war dead and the veterans of war by being silent as the ceremony is conducted. We stand quietly during the Silence and as the wreaths are placed. We also show respect by joining in the singing of our national anthem, "O Canada."

WHY SHOULD WE REMEMBER THEM?

We *remember* them to show that we are grateful for their sacrifices and their service to our country. We want to show them that today we appreciate that we live in a free and democratic country.

WHY DO WE SAY "LEST WE FORGET"?

We often see and hear these three words in reference to Remembrance Day. *Lest we forget* is a phrase from the poem "Recessional" written by Rudyard Kipling in 1897 for Queen Victoria's Diamond Jubilee (celebrating her 60th year as reigning monarch). In the poem, the words referred to the importance of remembering the sacrifice of Jesus Christ, but ever since the First World War, the phrase has been used to inspire us to remember, and to "never forget" the sacrifices made for us in war by these brave men and women.

On Remembrance Day, we remember "lest we forget." The Tomb of the Unknown Soldier, Ottawa, Ontario.

WHO ARE OUR VETERANS?

Military veterans are people who have served or are presently serving in the armed forces. On Remembrance Day, we honour these veterans who served and are still serving our country. One way we honour our veterans is by listening to the stories they tell us about their time in service to our country.

On Remembrance Day, we listen to the stories that our veterans share. Gordon McKenzie Hill (right) is a veteran of the Second World War.

A SECOND WORLD WAR REMEMBRANCE

Each veteran has his or her own stories about their war experiences. The following was told to me by one veteran of the Second World War, Flying Officer Gordon McKenzie Hill.

Gordon McKenzie Hill was born in Canora, Saskatchewan, on November 11, 1923. He lived on the family homestead with his parents, two sisters, and one brother. When he was growing up, during the Great Depression, he enjoyed riding his bike and playing baseball or kick the can. When his family moved to Regina, they lived near the airport, and young Gordon spent many hours watching the planes take off and land. When the Second World War began, Gordon saw the recruiting information for the armed forces on posters around town. Gordon knew he wanted to fly airplanes, and when he turned 18, he volunteered for the air force. He was trained and eventually became part of Squadron 416. Gordon flew a number of different planes, but mainly the Spitfire.

When his plane was shot by enemy fire over Germany on December 31, 1944, Gordon just managed to fly it back to friendly territory before it ran out of fuel. Each Remembrance Day, Gordon Hill remembers his many experiences during the war, both adventurous and frightening.

One month before the end of the war in Europe, Gordon visited the Belsen concentration camp. This visit is one of his worst memories from the war because he saw the bodies of many Jewish people and others who had been killed by the Nazis. At first he was sorry he had gone, but later, when some people questioned whether or not the Holocaust had happened, he knew it was true because he had seen it.

Gordon Hill lost many friends and colleagues during those years. Of those he worked with in daily operations, one person out of every three was killed. Of the eleven people he joined up with, only three returned home. On Remembrance Day, these many friends are a focus for his thoughts. And what are his thoughts about war? Well, he thinks that war is a terrible waste of people.

On Remembrance Day, we think about the young men and women who have served our country in times of war. (Left) Flying Officer Gordon McKenzie Hill.

THE TRUE NORTH STRONG AND FREE

HOW DO WE SHOW OUR CANADIAN PRIDE?

Canadians show pride in our country by flying our maple leaf flag. Flags are flown in public places, such as in front of schools and government buildings. Some people display a Canadian flag outside their home or business. On Remembrance Day, the flag is flown at half mast as a sign of respect for the fallen.

We also sing our national anthem, "O Canada." Most school assemblies and many public events begin with the singing of the anthem. It helps us to reflect on the fact that Canada is a wonderful country and reminds us of our duty to keep our land "glorious and free."

On Remembrance Day, we show pride in the accomplishments of our military men and women. They loved our country so much that they were willing to lay down their lives to protect it so that the Canadian way of life would continue. We show our pride by participating in Remembrance Day ceremonies and by remembering how fortunate we are to live in such a wonderful country.

Throughout our history, Canadians have been called on to stand up for freedom and the quest for freedom elsewhere. Many Canadians have made the ultimate sacrifice to ensure that we and others can live in freedom. For these Canadians and their families, it is a very difficult burden to bear.

Photo by Peter Creasey.

iStock/ © SkyF

On Remembrance Day, our Canadian pride is mixed with our sorrow for such great losses.

WHAT DOES IT MEAN TO BE CANADIAN?

Although it is difficult to put into words, there is a certain feeling that comes from being Canadian. We love our great northern land of diverse landscapes, incredible size, and people from every culture on the globe. We celebrate that in Canada we have freedom: freedom to do what we want within the law, freedom to believe what we want, and to say what we want. Canadians also proudly accept the responsibilities that go along with our freedom: to take care of ourselves and of one another, to remember that the feelings and needs of others matter in our quest for freedom, and to share our good gifts with the world.

On Remembrance Day, we think about what it means to be Canadian, and we show pride in our country. Here, the Canadian flag is being flown at half mast to honour our fallen.

A Quest for Peace

On Remembrance Day we honour those who have offered and given their lives in war, but it is important not to glorify war. In fact, it is the Canadian way to honour and work toward peace.

Each of us can make our own contribution to the quest for peace: peace in our hearts, peace with our friends, peace in our communities, and peace in the world. Canada as a country promotes peace in different ways and in many places across the world. Our armed forces have been involved in many peacekeeping operations organized by the United Nations over the years.

The Peace Tower

To demonstrate Canada's hope for peace, our government built a special structure known as the Peace Tower. The tower is part of the government building in Ottawa that also houses the House of Commons and the Senate.

The tower was completed in 1927, and, because it is so tall (more than 92 metres), it can easily be seen from almost anywhere in downtown Ottawa. The tower represents Canada's belief in itself as a country that seeks, protects, and promotes peace all over the world.

In the base of the Peace Tower is a very special room called the Memorial Chamber. The room is a tribute to the individuals who have lost their lives in war, and shows the respect that Canadians have for their war dead. Within the room are seven books, one for each of the war situations in which Canada has been involved. Each book contains the names of those Canadians who died in that conflict, and each name has been painstakingly printed in beautiful script. Every page in each of these books is opened for at least one day each year, so the names of every one of the fallen can be seen. Each day at 11:00 a.m. there is a ceremony in the Memorial Chamber at which the pages of these beautiful books are turned. It is significant that those who gave their lives in war have their names enshrined in the Peace Tower.

On Remembrance Day, we think about what we can do to help make our world a more peaceful one. It is our good thoughts and actions that can truly honour those who we remember, and make us worthy of their great sacrifice. (Right) The Peace Tower in Ottawa.

A Note from the Author

I am deeply grateful to Dundurn Press for publishing this book, which has truly been a labour of love on my part.

Several Dundurn staff members shared my vision and the work of preparing and making the book available. Special thanks are extended to: sales and marketing director Margaret Bryant, who believed enough to acquire the book and give me this grand opportunity; senior editor Allison Hirst, who engaged in a professional, knowledge-able, thoughtful, and considerate partnership that enabled us to make the book the best it could be; publicist Jim Hatch, who provided the expertise in helping to make the book available to its intended audience; and senior designer Courtney Horner and her design team, who made it look so good.

Thank you all!